AF471489

Raising Him

While He's Raising Me

Wonderful insight of how seeking God can impact the life of your child.

Beverly D. Jones

G~InSpired Publishing
Texas

 Printed in the United States of America. All scripture references are taken from the *King James Version Bible.*

For information, contact:
Inspirations By Beverly,
PO Box 330911, Fort Worth, Texas 76163

Beverly Jones
Raising Him While He's Raising Me
G~Inspired Publishing

ISBN 978-1-105-34069-7

First image on cover: Sergey Galushko ©, @ Fotolia
Second image on cover: kmit ©, @ Fotolia

Dedication

~

This book is dedicated to my amazing son.
You inspire me to be the very best that I can be.
I am so blessed to have you as my son.
I love you dearly.

Mom

Table of Contents

Introduction

~

Raising children is one of the most rewarding and fulfilling duties of a mother. Remember how you felt when your kids were born? Filled with an enormous amount of joy and excitement, you took them home with high hopes of a great future. Make no mistake, although enjoyable, motherhood is also taxing. As mothers, we have an assignment, a *task*, to cover and protect our children in prayer: the weapon in which God has given us.

Raising Him While He's Raising Me offers encouragement and hope as you mature in your calling as a single parent. In the midst of raising children, I believe it's vital to continue developing on a spiritual and emotional level in order to have the best mother-child experience possible.

My prayer is that you will benefit and share insights from this book with someone who's raising a son or daughter. I'm confident that this book will motivate you and those you love to raise tomorrow's leaders according to the plan of God.

Beverly D. Jones

Chapter One

Who Me? A Woman? Raise a Boy?

I'd like to say that I am *The Perfect Parent* and that I do all of the right things - *all of the time!* As you know, such a bold statement would be so far from the truth. I haven't met that person yet. Quite honestly, I will never meet that person. There are no perfect parents! There is no one who has created *"the patent"* on parenting. There are no ceremonial services where individuals receive "Flawless Parent of the Year Awards." Parenting is parallel to life in that we learn as we *grow*. There's no magic formula to assure us that we'll never make mistakes. There are no guarantees that things will always go right as we voyage through this fun-filled, sometimes unpredictable parent-child relationship. Long before having my son, I had thoughts of raising him in a great atmosphere. I imagined him not wanting for *anything!* I envisioned myself kissing all of his *boo-boos* away and somehow making all his pain disappear. I wanted him to be in the best environment possible. Never did the thought of raising him as a single parent enter my mind. I wanted the ideal situation. I wanted all of the circumstances to line up with my belief system. I wanted things to be...*perfect*! Well, I've discovered many things since that time.

Just as life is a journey, so is parenting. Life and parenting are both filled with joy and pain. They both come with lots of challenges and many surprises. Raising a boy has been a very humbling experience for me. Humbling because of the constant reminder that I'm not a male - I'm female. I'm different! I think differently! I act differently! It's a continuous trip to the throne room and many conversations with God. While humbling, raising a boy has also been inspiring for me. It's inspiring in the sense that I have become a better communicator and much more effective in my approach with life's unexpected issues. Keeping it simple and less dramatic has proven to leave more of an impact! During this amazing journey, I've seen how my prayer life has taken on a whole new meaning. Over the years, my prayers have transformed from the infant stages of, *"Lord, help me to always be there for my son,"* to a more mature prayer that I believe all wise parents must pray, *"Lord, teach me to let him go."* It doesn't mean that I care any less as he grows taller and his voice transforms into this *deep, unfamiliar sound.* Development is progressive, and while my son is changing physically, he is also maturing into a great product of what he's been taught from the time he was very young. My son and I are in a different season of life and some of the things that use to work when he was smaller no longer works.

As my son first began to grow older, I remember going through a period of feeling *left out.* I noticed that he stopped sharing *everything* with me. I remember on several occasions, in the afternoons or evenings when I'd ask my son Overton how his day went. He consistently answered with one word, "*good.*" It was almost as if he were saying, "Isn't that how you expected my day to go?" I wanted him to elaborate more on how his day went. I wanted him to share the intricate details and not just render some vague answer to appease me for the moment. I wanted him to *tell all - leaving nothing out!* I wanted more than just the highlights of his day. Women, you understand! What I've come to realize is that it's unusual for the average boy to be talkative. There are times when a girl may be plagued because of an incident that took place in her life. She doesn't mind sharing _all_ of the details. She may even become emotional. What does a boy do? In most cases, he will do something totally opposite. Showing little or no emotions, he will just shake it off, move on, and his world continues as normal. Typically, boys do not go around spilling their guts or expressing themselves in the same manner as girls. This can sometimes create a communication barrier between a mother and son. As a mother, what I'm learning is that, in some instances, we need to connect with God in order to connect with them.

Even though they've inherited traits from both sides of the coin (from mother and father), and we *think* we know why they do what they do or feel the way they feel, we sometimes have to consult with God on how to handle certain situations. It's deeper than what we sometimes think or say; "He's just acting like his Father," or "Why didn't he get my better qualities?" While our children are a mixture of both mom and dad, let's not forget that they were also crafted by the hands of God as spiritual beings. They were designed by God and sent to earth with a purpose. So, in our prayer time, we should always bring them before God. Not only does God see the bigger picture, He created the *bigger* picture for *His purpose*. Satan also knows that your son has purpose and a great future established by God. That's why it is so important to seek God on behalf of our children – *daily.*

Remember when your son was an infant and you'd wrap him in those cute little pastel blankets? They were so soft and snugly. Some were even designed with cartoon characters. These blankets may have been appealing to the eye or maybe even humorous depending on the characters you selected. However, the look and style of the blanket was secondary. Your main purpose was to shield your child from the wind and the elements in order to prevent any type of sickness or discomfort. You also wanted him to feel the warmth of your love and give him a sense of protection. No matter the age or stage of our children, we can still wrap them in a blanket of protection. Your kids may be a lot bigger now, maybe even adults, but they can remain covered. God has given us a powerful defense mechanism to safeguard them: prayer. Every child needs it - *and lots of it*! I believe our duty as parents is to pray for our children. We simply cannot afford to escape this assignment from God.

Who's at Risk?

Becoming a single parent years ago was very intimidating for me. Thoughts of failure and unanswered questions constantly bombarded my mind. I remember asking God, "How am I going to raise a boy all by myself?" This question kept echoing in the crevices of my mind. My son, who was five at the time, loved both his dad and me. Rightfully so, after all, we are the parents that God blessed him with. Looking at my son with tears in my eyes and feelings of helplessness, I'd ask myself, "How will he turn out?" "How will the divorce impact him?" I had so many questions. During this time, I would hear statements that associated children from single parent homes at a greater risk for gang violence, becoming school dropouts, and engaging in drug activities. In many households, this was a reality! Isn't it amazing how Satan presents negative information to us sometimes during the lowest moments in our lives? I am so glad that I did not buy into that lie! The truth of the matter is that all kids are at risk! They're at risk whether they've come from the most affluent neighborhoods or an underprivileged community. This includes all ethnicities as well as kids from two parent homes. There is no preference when it comes to Satan. He wants to destroy our kids while they are young. Plain and simple! Remember the story of the children of Israel? Pharaoh wanted to kill all of the male children under the age of two. Why? To stop their destiny! He wanted to prevent them from moving forward in order to further his agenda. He wanted to stop the plan of God. Satan does not like you as a woman because of your ability to give life nor does he like your son who has the ability to manifest his intended *purpose of life.* In fact, he hates us.

"And his tail drew the third part of the stars of heaven, and did cast them to the earth: and the dragon stood before the woman which was ready to be delivered, for to devour her child as soon as it was born."

Revelation 12:4, KJV

Satan is seeking to grab our kids anyway he can. He wants to destroy them right now! It is so vital that we walk in wisdom. We should also understand that his plan of destruction is not always a physical death. Instead, he takes pleasure in destroying their trust in the very people that should protect them. He enjoys robbing them of their innocence and leaving them here to wallow in pity, guilt, and sometimes self-destructive behavior. When this happens, their purpose is neglected and many lives go untouched as they stumble in an attempt to find themselves and their meaning of existence. The good news is that the grace of God can restore them back to their true identity.

Assume Your Role

Our children are facing so many things in school and society. Bullying is at an all time high and has taken on a whole new meaning. Kids today are not only dealing with the type of bullying that may turn into a physical scuffle or an exchange of blows on the school playground. This is what took place when I was growing up. In most cases, issues were addressed and settled on the playground.

Today, many kids are dealing with *cyber bullying*. What's interesting about cyber bullying is that many times there's no physical threat. Cyber bullying can be done through cell phone texting, online, or other technical methods. A cyber bully can just simply tell the victim they're ugly or that they're not good enough. The victim believes them and starts to feel that they "do not belong". They may also experience some type of character assassination from a cyber bully. The victim becomes entangled in a *"web"* of anxiety and will sometimes *self-destruct*. While there may not be a physical threat, the bully has marked their subject with fear and terror. Bullying is serious and should not be taken lightly. You know it's serious when studies have shown that a large percentage of boys who were known as bullies by their first year of high school end up committing crimes and having convictions by the age of twenty four years old. Mothers, we've got to get serious with our first commission: to save our home - our children.

Drug abuse by the youth is also widespread. I know many kids are inquisitive and they just want to know what it *feels like* to get 'high'. Many of them want to look cool and just fit in. I believe some things should just simply be left *undiscovered.* We all know what curiosity did to the cat.

I cannot emphasize enough how we **must** keep them covered in prayer. Not only is peer pressure a factor, but we must also remain alert even with the educators and those of authority in their lives. I've had the pleasure of establishing some good relationships with many of my son's teachers. I believe that some of them are actually *called* to teach and love what they do. Great teachers still exist and I applaud them for their diligence and commitment. It certainly does make up for those teachers who have abused their authority and have manipulated those entrusted to them. You've seen the news; many educators with distorted beliefs displaying perverted behavior toward their students. During the early part of 2011, a school teacher in the Texas area turned herself in to authorities after she was accused of having sex with five students in her home. This is the type of news no parent enjoys hearing! While we do not want to walk in paranoia and fear, we must shield our children with the Word of God!

I am so thankful to my mother for openly displaying the importance of prayer in my life as a child. She demonstrated the significance of praying to God on a regular basis. She has truly passed on a legacy of prayer. As a child, I witnessed my mother praying daily over my siblings and me. On numerous occasions, I remember seeing her talking to God standing at the kitchen sink while looking out of the window. If I didn't know any better, I would've thought there was someone in there with her. I'd walk in the kitchen and sense the presence of God so strongly. It was obvious that she had a relationship with God and was definitely a force to be reckoned with in the spirit. Before my siblings and I would go to school, my mother would gather us in a circle and pray. We knew that whatever we faced on any given day that God was with us. I remember feeling like a conqueror whenever my mother prayed with us. An overwhelming sense of confidence would rise up in me. These experiences created unforgettable memories that I will always treasure.

I know we want to give our children material things, resources, and a better life than what we had. Undoubtedly, it is rewarding to see your children blessed. No other feeling can compare when their countenance is illuminated by a gift purchased just for them. What joy to see them obtaining knowledge and gaining the riches that can be acquired on this earth! Along with attaining worldly gratification, why not also leave them a legacy of prayer? Why not leave them with an inheritance of knowing their rights as a believer in Christ and teaching them how to walk in authority over Satan?

Mothers, instead of lying in bed until the very last second while your kids scramble for backpacks and unfinished homework assignments, why not take a moment and pray over them in the mornings? Perhaps read a scripture over them or have them read. Just think of the impact in our schools if we'd stop and recognize the importance of raising God-fearing kids *(And all the teachers said amen!).* They are indeed our future! This is more than a cliché. We are sending our children into the world in hopes that they would escape the dangers of life and somehow arrive to their destinations unscathed. Yes, it's true; they will encounter those who will fight against them. They will run up against the wolf in sheep's clothing. All of this is okay if we have prepared and covered them with God's weaponry. The problem is that so many kids are leaving home uncovered and open to the schemes of their greatest enemy: Satan. Over the years, the following scripture has become so real to me.

"No weapon that is formed against thee shall prosper…"
Isaiah 54:17, KJV

I believe there is power in that scripture! Weapons may be created and produced to come against us, but they WILL NOT PROSPER! The blood of Jesus protects us from all danger - seen and unseen. It also protects us from accusations - from the lies of the enemy. My son may not completely understand it all, but he knows that before he opens the front door, a prayer will be prayed, a scripture will be read or quoted, and the blood of Jesus will be spoken over him. I want him to know that it's real and it works! I believe those prayers of my mother have spared my life from the traps of the enemy many times over. I know that she is still praying for me. She exercised her role as a mother by instilling in her kids that we can always go to God in prayer.

Yes, I'm a single parent raising my son, but I am no longer tormented with the fear of raising a boy into a powerful man of God. As you read further, you'll see that it takes God and humbling yourself in order to be productive and effective. I may be a single parent, but I am not alone and neither are you.

Notes

Notes

Chapter Two

Get a Grip – He's Watching You!

"Train up a child in the way he should go, and when he is old, he will not depart."

Proverbs 22:6, KJV

How many times have you heard, "Kids are resilient"? This is true. Kids are sometimes a lot tougher than what we give them credit for. They certainly are more forgiving than most adults. Given the right circumstances and environment, children can recover and spring back into *normality,* even after tragic events.

After my twelve years of marriage ended, my son and I briefly went to live with my mother. I remember on one particular cold winter day, my son and I were home alone. He was playing with his toys in the tiny bedroom that we both shared. I excused myself into the hallway and sat on the floor. I was crying, or should I say, "Forcing myself to cry," *and somewhat loudly*. I was feeling sorry for myself.

On that day, pity and I had an appointment. I showed up! And what a party we had! I wanted to relish in this time of sadness; after all, I'd been through a lot, so I wanted my moment. I earned it and I deserved it! What a distorted way of thinking.

I've never been a person that tried to gain attention in a negative way, but on this particular day, I wanted my son to see me. I wanted him to hear me – to feel my pain! I wanted to bring him into this party of despair. I had a plan! While sitting there on the floor, I had a vision that he'd hear me and come pat me on the back and say, "Are you okay mommy?" I imagined him hugging me, perhaps running to get some tissue and wiping those hard-earned tears away, as I would just sit there and cry. Well…thank God he didn't hear me!

My son was five at the time, and when he was indulged in playing, he couldn't hear a thing! He's an only child and was used to playing alone most of the time, so it was nothing for him to hold conversations with these lifeless objects. He'd crash them to the floor while making thunderous noises with his mouth. He was the typical boy! He'd sometimes sing or hum while playing. Needless to say, he never knew that I was on the hallway floor feeling sorry for myself. He never knew that I was trying to manipulate him to come and *rescue me – to save me.* He never heard me!

Someone Heard Me

After I quickly discovered that my son didn't hear me and wasn't coming to my rescue, someone else heard me. **"GET A GRIP – HE'S WATCHING YOU!"** said this voice. [Not quite the voice I had in mind]. Remember, I wanted to hear the gentle, innocent voice of my son asking me if I were okay. Instead, I heard the spirit of God speak to me. **A loving BUT Firm Voice! A Precise Command!**

It didn't take long before I stopped crying, dried my tears, and rose from the floor. Was God upset with my crying? Was He acting like the typical male chauvinist wondering, "Why can't you just get it together?"

Absolutely Not! My crying did not bother God; after all, He bottles up every tear we shed and *is* touched by our pain. Even though I was hurting emotionally and certainly could have used someone's shoulder to cry on, I'm sure God did not appreciate the way that I attempted to gain my son's attention. Besides, my son was hurting also and wanted things to be *normal* again. My son could not give me the peace or satisfaction that I longed for at that particular moment.

He's My Confidence

What I have learned since that time is how important it is to cry out to God. It's really okay to open up to Him in times of weakness. In Him, we find comfort, guidance, and strength. For each time we cry out to God, there is an exchange. For our sadness, He gives joy. Instead of confusion, He offers peace. When there is lack, He supplies all your needs. God has truly been my anchor. In seeking God, we begin to transform more into His image and gain the character and confidence we need. The moral fibers of our lives begin to line up with the words that He's already declared over us. After diligently seeking Him, I've seen how my confidence has soared over the years. I praise God for His Word. His Word is life changing and absolute! His Word will never change! Yes, I still cry, but I cry out to the One who can help me.

As I look back over my life, I thank Him for the people He's allowed to come into my path over the past nine years. There have been those who were in my life for a season and have moved on but their lives served a purpose at a time when I needed them the most. Some of them have imparted valuable treasure inside me and I am now seeing the fruits of their labor. Through their obedience and life experiences, I was able to glean from them and gain self-confidence to meet life head on. There were also those who I call *distracters*, but I'll give them credit too. Their purpose was to also make me a better person. I learned that God uses every circumstance, the good - the bad - the different – those for you - those against you, to build your character and confidence *in Him.* Those who know me well also know that people do not easily intimidate me. This confidence has come after many years of hardship and simply trusting God. I praise God for what He has done in me!

When my son looks at me, I want him to see an example of what confidence is. I want him to see someone who is poised and knows how to keep it together. I want him to see a gentle, loving mother and yet have him identify with the inner strength that comes from his Heavenly Father. Our children are watching us! God has commanded us as parents to teach our children according to His Word. God's Word should be a part of our daily lives and not just a temporary antidote when problems arise.

"And thou shalt teach them diligently unto thy children, and shalt talk of them when thou sittest in thine house, and when thou walkest by the way, and when thou liest down, and when thou risest up."

Deuteronomy 6:7, KJV

According to this particular verse, we should always share the Word of God with our children. Does that mean to only discuss the Word of God and nothing else? Absolutely not, but it does mean that we are to be mindful of His Word when we're interacting with our children. We are to share the goodness of God with them. One thing that I do with my son is compare God's Word with circumstances and things that are going on in our lives. I really try to keep it relative and balanced so that he will understand. God's Word is refreshing. It brings life to any situation. When my son has a challenge, I remind him of certain scriptures. I remind him that he's already victorious. One of my favorite scriptures for him is, **"I can do all things through Christ which strengtheneth me." Philippians 4:13, KJV.** This is one verse that is used regularly in our spiritual artillery. I often remind my son of Bible characters who were confronted with obstacles and yet overcame them. God's Word is life and can help us in *any* situation.

Over the years, my son has seen me in many facets of life. He's seen me cry out to God in troubled times and has witnessed God's deliverance each and every time. He has seen and experienced the favor of God in our lives on many occasions. Years ago, God began dealing with me about becoming more of a giver. I began teaching my son the importance of giving, and as a result, he is more giving. I've witnessed his compassion and sensitivity when he hears of someone who may be in need. I do not want him to become a man always looking for a handout. I want him to act on God's prompting so that when he sees a need – he is *willing and able* to respond. It is important to me that he lives by the words… **"It is more blessed to give than to receive." Acts 20:35, KJV**

Over time, I've asked myself many questions. What do I want my son to see when he's looking at me? Do I want him to see me as a weak woman who's afraid to stand up to life? Do I want him to see me out of control when I do not get my way? Do I want him to think that it's okay to have a "take it or leave it" attitude concerning the Word of God? Absolutely Not!

What do you want your son to see when looking at you? Do you want him to see a person with low self-esteem who's afraid to look people in their faces? Do you want him to see you in a constant battle of depression? Do you want your son to become a replica of the “real you”? Go to God with a sincere heart and ask Him for help. He will hear you! Ask God to heal you emotionally and then start seeking Him through His Word. One thing I know for sure is that God’s Word brings healing and life.

God has placed these special people we call sons in our lives for us to not only nurture but also equip them for the many battles that lie ahead. We cannot put them down or speak negative words over them and somehow expect them to become great men of society or powerful men of God. By nature, my son has acquired some of my characteristics. Beyond that, I want him to see me on a deeper level. What do I want my son to see when he’s watching me? I want him to see the spirit of Christ who lives in me!

Notes

Notes

Chapter Three

Thou Hast Been My Help

"Hide not thy face far from me; put not thy servant away in anger: thou hast been my help; leave me not, neither forsake me, O God my salvation."

Psalm 27:9, KJV

After becoming a single parent, this scripture above became so precious to me. I've relied on this verse in the course of God developing my faith in Him. One thing I have discovered is that God is my deliverer and has remained a constant factor in my life. Even in my unfaithfulness to Him, He's remained faithful to me. I didn't grow up with a father in the home. My mother was a single parent also. While my father lived in the same city as me, he never cultivated a relationship with me. I remember longing for a relationship with my father at the age of thirty-three years old. I was praying for God to mend my heart of the many disappointments and hurts that I had experienced up to that point.

I wanted some sense of satisfaction and acceptance. I wanted to know what true love really was. I wanted to experience unconditional love from a man, in this case, *my father*. I wanted to know what it felt like to have someone love me without any hidden motives. I wanted to experience the joy of knowing that my father was proud of me. I've never received that type of love or recognition from my natural father.

God Accepts Me

Over the years, I've come to realize that it doesn't matter where I came from, who left me, who hurt me, or who does not approve of me. God has made it very clear that He loves me for who I am. He made me! **He made me and I am His!** He created me for greatness! In fact, I have greatness inside of me because He lives in me. I'm no longer looking for validation from anyone! God has stamped me with His approval – even while being formed in my mother's womb. I am the apple of God's eye! I am already accepted in the beloved! I'm accepted - even in the midst of disappointments, failures, and setbacks. God is my father, the ultimate dad, the one who loves me unconditionally. Jesus is my savior, my knight in shining armor. He protects me and has rescued me from my enemies. I'm never alone because the Holy Spirit communes with me and guides my footsteps along the right paths. Sure, I make mistakes, but God's love for me is everlasting and immutable.

We can rely on the One who will never leave us. We do not have to create a performance to receive God's love. We can be who we are without pretending. He wants us to come before Him – boldly and unashamed, yet humble and obedient. We do not have to wear the labels that others have placed on us. That's why He is the ultimate Father because we can boldly approach Him with any concerns in our hearts.

We never have to fear that He will turn us away because we're "*not good enough.*" He owns everything, so He'll never say, "*I wish that I had the money to help you out.*" Jesus is the prince of peace, so we'll never hear Him say, "*I have too much on my mind right now - come back later, and we'll talk.*" No! He is with you, to help in *your* time of trouble. God is there for you at this very moment. Call on Him.

While a close-knit relationship with my natural father would have been nice, I am so thankful for a relationship with my heavenly father. Through the years, God has manifested Himself in so many ways. He's been my provider, healer, comforter, friend, protector - and the list goes on.

As a child, I grew up in a church denomination where we had a certain time blocked out during each church service for those who wanted to stand up and share the goodness of God. We called it *"testimony service."* Well, in this chapter, I simply want to *testify* and be a witness of the Lord's goodness. God has turned many impossible situations around for me. I hope these testimonies encourage you in whatever circumstances you may be facing today.

My Provider

Years ago, I was sitting in church along with my son and my eldest sister on a Sunday morning. In walks a lady and is seated to the left of me. She and I began talking about the goodness of the God. We worshipped the Lord in a very anointed service. When the service ended, this lady asked me to sit down. I sat down, and she began to write a check. She said the Lord instructed her to write a personal check made payable to me for a particular amount. Prior to this moment, I had never seen this lady in my life. In fact, she and her family had just moved to the Dallas-Fort Worth area at that time. She handed me the check, and to my astonishment, it was written for over eight hundred dollars. As I walked through the church parking lot, back to the car, my sister and I marveled in how God performed such a miracle. There was a great need for this money! Not only was it a blessing for me but also to my sister who had a desperate need at that time. This was one of those *WOW* moments and certainly a divine appointment set by God. My God is faithful!

He Keeps On Providing

One period of my life, I went through a season of job lay offs and knew all to well what it felt like to have the bills pile up. At one point, I was facing eviction. My rent was about two and a half months past due along with late fees. After going to several public agencies and those who I thought would help, I was left empty handed. Despite this, I believed God would come through for me. Was it easy? No, but it taught me a lot. Through this experience, I learned how to trust God. I had to lean on Him like never before. At that time, the Word of God was more important to me than *anything or anyone*. My son and I were supposed to have moved out on December 15th of that year – exactly ten days before Christmas. The constable had already served the eviction papers. In man's eyes, it was a done deal. The funny thing about it all was that I never felt led to pack up and move. I didn't pack anything! I knew that God was coming through for me, but I didn't know how. During this process, I mentioned what I was going through to a dear friend. I merely told her so that she could pray and agree with me. Besides, she had her own set of financial issues at the time. On the evening of December 14th, this same friend was knocking at my door. It wasn't a normal knock. It was a knock of urgency! When I opened the door, she placed two checks on my sofa and said my rent was paid. That week, God had blessed her with two unexpected checks totaling more than what I needed plus the two hundred dollars that I had. She took the money that I had along with those two checks she received and bought a cashier's check the next day, and I was able to pay my landlord on December 15th. God came through! Every time I think of this, tears flow down my face and I experience an overwhelming moment of gratitude toward God for His faithfulness.

The stories just go on and on. There was another time while I was driving that a lady hit my car from behind. She and her husband called me and wanted to make arrangements to pay me cash. There was hardly any damage done to my car (just a scratch or two). Well, the very next day, this couple brought five hundred dollars to my house. The timing could not have been better because there was a need for this money. God is so creative! He allowed her to hit my car but not harm my son or me in order to supply a need. Going through those experiences taught me to trust God. I also learned to appreciate and honor the gifts and talents that He had placed inside of me. We have to walk in the confidence that God is our source. He has many ways to bless you aside from traditional resources. **But my God shall supply all your need according to his riches in glory by Christ Jesus." Philippians 4:19, KJV**

My Protection

A few years ago, my son and I were living in a nice duplex in a *not-so-nice neighborhood.* At one time, there were people living next door to us who weren't so *neighborly* nor did they respect other people's privacy or property. One night, after midnight, I was headed for bed when my telephone rang. It was a friend. She said that the Lord placed me on her heart and felt she needed to call. While talking with her, I walked to my living room window and looked out of my blinds. I saw two young men (one being my neighbor) headed towards the back of our duplex. It looked as though they were trying to break in. When one man discovered me looking out of the window, they quickly ran back to their side of the duplex. Needless to say, I called the police and never had any more problems out of them. Just imagine if my friend had not obeyed the voice of God. What if she hadn't called me? What if I had not looked out of the window at the right time? I am a firm believer in Psalm 121 and Psalm 91. God will watch over your life even when you are not aware of the dangers and traps set by Satan. You'd better believe that I earnestly sought the Lord, and those neighbors were eventually forced to move.

There are so many times when God has come through for me. If I were to have written them all, you would have probably placed the book down by now. There would be too many pages.

The truth of the matter is we all have a testimony. I know God has come through for you and you too have stories to tell. Maybe you are feeling depressed, worried, and can see no way out. I want to remind you that God will come through for you regardless of the situation. I can't tell you how He will deliver you or when it will happen. I can tell you that He will give you peace in the midst of your storm. He cares about everything that concerns you. He is the God of this universe and He wants to be your Father. If He is not your Father, then let's just pause for a moment, and you can accept Him in your heart right now. God wants an intimate relationship with you, and it starts with you receiving Him as Lord of your life.

Pray this prayer aloud…

"Father, I believe you are God. I believe you sent your son, Jesus, to die for my sins. I believe that He rose from the grave and that He lives forevermore. I confess there's a void in me that I've tried to fill with other things. Forgive me of all my sins. I accept you into my heart and life as my Lord and Savior. I believe you have purpose for my life. I believe that I am saved and free of all sin. I am your child - in Jesus name. Amen."

Wow! You are now saved. You are a child of God! You are born again! I'll be honest with you, your problems may not disappear right away, but I guarantee that God will help you. He's with you right now!

Whether you started at chapter one or if you just turned to this particular page, God knew you would be reading this book at this moment. He loves you so much that He allowed you to confess this prayer and accept Him as your Lord. He is your Father, and you can go to Him in prayer *anytime* you need Him. It's that simple. He will help you!

Notes

Notes

Chapter Four

Like It or Not!

I believe it's safe to say that you as a parent want the very best for your son. Or, do you? Now, before you raise that *one* eyebrow or say, "Who do you think you are?" "Of course I want the best for my son," read further. By the end of this chapter, I want you to honestly evaluate yourself and then answer that question. Fair enough?

As a single parent, I've had my share of many difficult moments. In fact, it's been down right hard at times. From bearing the load of sole provider, short-orders cook, all the way to an M.D. That doesn't stand for medical doctor. It stands for one Mad D… woman!

I went through a period where I was mad with my ex-husband because of his lack of involvement in raising our son. Now, before moving on, I must say this chapter is not about bashing my son's father or making him look bad. He now spends a lot more time with our son, and I've seen how God has transformed their relationship. Could things be better? Of course, but I'm thankful for the change that I see right now. Let's take a moment and be thankful for the fathers who are involved with their sons and spend quality time with them.

Character Building

I was MAD – Very Mad! I had many questions. "How does he get off so free?" "Why doesn't he spend time with his son?" "Why won't he do this?" "Why won't he do that?" My all-time favorite was, "Why doesn't he help me financially?" I'd then follow up with a *very* demeaning statement. *Well…I'll just let you use your imagination.*

Isn't it amazing how God works? He will allow people to come into your life at the right time to help guide you along. During this time, He blessed me with the right person to get me through this very difficult season. I called her my spiritual mother at the time. Boy, did she get an ear full! She heard me cry, complain, and cry some more. I remember on several occasions, I'd remind her of how tough it was and how I was not getting any financial support from my son's father. I'd often tell her that my son and I didn't deserve this. She'd listen so patiently and attentively. This went on for a while. I would complain and say things about him that were not pleasing to God. I was never a person that used bad language, but I certainly got my point across! When I was done with my crab session, she'd chime in and often say in a calm voice, "God is building your character." *"Excuse Me?!" "Building my character?!" "How much character am I lacking?!" "How much more do I need?!"* Yes, these were a few of the many questions and verbal expressions that I had for her. Remember, **I was MAD!**

"And not only so, but we glory in tribulations also; knowing that tribulation worketh patience; And patience, experience; and experience, hope."

Romans 5:3-4, KJV

She would remind me of God's Word. She would also say things like, "he may be the father of your son, but he is not your source – God is your source." Oh….how that disturbed me at first! In my mind, I would question, "Are you my friend or not – who's side are you really on?" Ladies, let me tell you something. God was working on me! I felt that I was in a "Tribulation Worketh Patience –

It's Not About You Anyway" boot camp. God had me in severe training. While experiencing life's challenges, let's be mindful that we should grow and become better in the process. There is much to gain in the midst of our testing. Our *"going through"* isn't about us anyway. It's for the people we are to minister to who are coming behind us. If we persevere, in faith, we will get what He's promised! God was truly molding my character. As I look back and have grown to understand, God was healing the very core of my being. I needed emotional, mental, and spiritual healing. He took an ugly situation, a dark moment of my life, and started something new! He helped me to see that I was a woman of worth. A woman of quality! It didn't look like it at the moment. I was emotionally worn. The inner turmoil I experienced was sometimes overwhelming. My physical appearance was also impacted. I was experiencing facial breakouts. My hair was falling out. I was at an all time low! I had seen better days before then. I was a mess, but God is so awesome!

Although I am still a work in progress, I've seen how God has transformed me more into His image. I often think if I had not allowed Him to change me, what a negative impact this would've had on my son TODAY!

Change the Root - Change What You Produce

I could not allow the way that I was feeling to continue to dominate or defeat me. I remember praying early on, "Lord, do not allow me to become bitter." Even though I went through a period of anger, my spirit would not allow bitterness to take root. I began speaking to the broken places in my life. I had to allow God to begin the healing process so that I could effectively raise my son. I didn't want to see him grow up as a depleted soul scarred by his mother's lack of forgiveness. He needed to know who he was in Christ. I didn't have to remind him of what his dad and I had gone through or how hurt I felt.

It was time to leave the past behind and allow God to shift our lives in another direction. As God was healing me, I began ministering to my son. I was calling things forth in his life, speaking into his future and destiny. I began speaking to the broken places in my son. As parents, we cannot be selfish; we have to remember that our kids are people with feelings and a future – a destiny. They need us, and more importantly, they need our prayers! So, whatever pleasure you think you are getting from holding on to the past - let it go. Be free!

The Beginning of Change

While going through this process, I was instructed to pray for my son's father. "Pray for him - are you kidding me?!" By this time, I didn't know what to think of my spiritual mom. Now, prior to meeting my spiritual mother, I had prayed for a seasoned woman of God to come into my life. I prayed for a spiritual mentor. I really believe God brought her into my life at that particular time. She was very sedate and always answered in a tranquil manner – totally opposite of me, *at that time*. God really does answer prayer. After she told me to start praying for my son's father, I began to think, "She doesn't know what she's talking about." Well, as it turns out, she knew exactly what she was talking about.

She encouraged me to use my mouth to *bless* him and not *curse* him. She didn't mean to *not* use profanity when he and I communicated. She meant to speak positive words over my son's father – over his life. You'd think that she would have understood and left me alone (but she really did understand). It took a while for me to even muster a prayer for him and be sincere in doing so. Like it or not, I did it, and over the years, it's gotten easier. Not only has praying for him brought healing to me but it's also been a blessing for my son to experience. I remember the first time that I called out his father's name in prayer (in the presence of my son), and a look of shock and curiosity came over his face. My son knows that I am a passionate person who stands strongly for what I believe in. So when my son heard that prayer, I believe he knew that a change had come. Praying for his dad was not something that I mastered overnight, but it certainly was the beginning.

More Change

"And He shall turn the heart of the fathers to the children, and the heart of the children to their fathers..."

Malachi 4:6, KJV

I had another person in my life for a season that encouraged me to pray for the relationship between my son and his father. God was really lining things up. By this time, I was in another place, spiritually. I have to admit that this was a lot easier to do because I knew that my son could only benefit from spending time with his dad. Let's face it, mothers; we can only give so much, but a boy needs his father or perhaps a good male role model in his life. I literally began praying the Word of God over their relationship. It did not happen instantly, but God's Word worked. Their relationship is something I never could have imagined during my tug-of-war with God to just *simply pray*. I did not have to manipulate or control the situation. I simply yielded myself to the spirit of God and toward the instructions of women who were obviously being used by God.

Young women, hear me. You need a trusted mature woman of God in your life. In most cases, she may not be your best friend, but she will be an asset to you. It's okay to have someone to talk to, to pray with, and to guide you. Just make sure God has sent her to you. We need an outlet. Do not make the mistake in allowing your son to become a sounding board for your frustrations about *his father*. He adores his dad and looks up to him. Let him have that! You never know, your son may be praying and could be the reason for the turn around in his father's life. If your son is hurt and disappointed in his dad right now, and if he refuses to talk with you about the situation, this is when *you* cry out to God. This is an opportunity for you to seek God's healing for your son and yes, pray for his dad. Remember, it's okay to cry out to God in times of need.

I believe it is vital to pray for the other parent even when they are not involved as they should be. In fact, that's all the more reason to pray. You must pray – even when it doesn't feel good! Your child will benefit! He will see the act of forgiveness at work in you, which will bless him. *He'll need to see that because he will also need to forgive you at some point.* Maybe your situation is different from mine. Perhaps the other parent is incarcerated, on drugs, or just not actively involved in your child's life for many reasons. Whatever the reason, and if the other parent is still alive, free yourself. Forgive him. Let your son see God at work in you! My son has witnessed me praying for his dad, and I believe this has inspired him to pray also.

From a Bitter Parent to a Bigger Purpose

Women, we have complained about men and how they treat us or how they do not treat us. Yes it's true; there's a lot of disrespect in many male-female relationships. Why continue adding to this insanity? Let's instill in our sons the benefits of loving God, respecting their parents, and producing great men that will improve society and grow the kingdom of God. You may ask, "Why should I pray for the person who hurt me so badly and refuse to involve himself with the responsibilities of parenting?" Think of it this way. If you remain bitter and continue to pour this acid into your son, you will stifle his growth and he will not reach his full potential. He'd only offer those in his inner circle a small percentage of what God has placed inside of him. Imagine if you would allow God to heal you emotionally and see how your child could impact a community or possibly the world. In doing this, you would give him the opportunity to fulfill his purpose.

Far too often, I see bitter mothers raising sons with high expectations of them, expecting them to grow up and become something great. You've seen it too. Not you of course! How many times have we heard *other* women say things like, "Oh…my baby is going to grow up and make mama proud?" "He's going to be a doctor, a lawyer, a professional athlete, a judge, or the president!" Yes, they can become any of these great men and *many have*. We see many athletes and great men of stature from single parent homes, including our current president, achieve great success. We rush our sons to grow up, make something of their lives, make lots of money, and when they marry insecure and shallow wives, we're upset. This is so hypocritical!

A mirror only reflects what it sees. How can we expect them to marry anything other than what they've become accustomed to? How can we expect greatness of our children if we've injected them with the toxins from our past? Your son has purpose; he has a destiny to reach. He has lives to change. Do not hold him back! Let him see you in a whole new light. I'd rather my son observe me reaching for greatness and sometimes failing than for him to see me master misery and mediocrity.

A Son's Love – A Father's Touch

I've never minimized the significance of my role as a mother. By nature, we mothers have an inner ability to nurture and avail ourselves to our children as they need us. Even with great intentions, we must be careful to not stifle or *baby* them, particularly our sons. As a teenager, my son still needs me. He needs the tenderness of my love but without smothering him. I have to let him grow, breathe, and become all that God has called him to be.

As I began to see God work in the relationship between him and his father, I had to take a step back. Early on, I remember seeing my son's eyes light up in the presence of his father. It brought me joy to see the love he displayed for his dad. There are some things that only a man can give to a boy. Who better than for a father to impart to a son and bless him?

"By faith Jacob, when he was dying, blessed both the sons of Joseph…" Hebrews 11:21, KJV

If there is an area where my son needs help and I'm not able to meet that need, I've learned to pray for him. Before discussing my concerns with his dad, I sometimes pray first. Depending on the issue or situation, I pray that God enlightens the eyes of his father and gives him wisdom to meet that need. It's a feeling of satisfaction, and we all benefit. His dad benefits by walking in his role as a father; I benefit by walking in forgiveness and my son reaps the rewards of receiving love and support from the both of us.

It's natural for a son to desire his father's love. Several years ago, during my angry period with my son's father, I had a deep desire for him to see the importance of spending quality time with our son. As they began spending more time with each other, I remember feeling a little left out. They'd go to the movies or their favorite eating place, particularly for ice cream. At one point, I started to feel that my son didn't love me as much. I'm sure God was thinking, "Woman, make up your mind, do you want the man in his life or not?" Mothers, allow your sons to love their fathers. It's okay! Do not interrupt what God is doing in their relationship. As I've come to realize that my son loves me no less – just differently. It's emotional balance for him – to share the love that he has for the both of us. I give God praise for being patient with me. I thank Him for change! I did not like *how* He was changing me, but over time, it has all worked together for the good.

Now back to my original question. Do you really want the best for your son? Are you speaking words of life over your son's father? Are you blessing or cursing him? Does your answer line up with your actions? Like it or not – Let God change YOU!

My Prayer for You…

"Father, bless the woman reading this book. Help her to know that she is special and that you love her with an everlasting love. Go to the very core of her being and heal her emotionally and cause her to rise tall and live in your joy. In Jesus Name - Amen."

Notes

Notes

Chapter Five

Worth The Sacrifice

"A little bit today, a little bit tomorrow - Time well spent with no sorrow
He'll be grown up, sooner than you think - In an instant if your eyes were to blink
Cherish each moment as if it were a prize - Years will slip by before you realize
Do it all over again, you ask, would I? - My, oh my, I would oblige."

~ Beverly D. Jones ~

When I look at my son, who is now a teenager, I think about how the years have come and gone. I remember when he was much smaller and saying to my friends, "I have a long way to go." My son and I have experienced so much together: memories of seeing him graduate from kindergarten, late night trips to the emergency room, and numerous spelling bee victories. Now, I get the pleasure of journeying with him as he pursues the goals that God has outlined for him. A mother's love, strength, and support are beyond belief. One thing I have discovered since the birth of my son is how selflessly and willingly mothers sacrifice for their children.

As mothers, it's not hard to give of ourselves for the betterment of our children. God has entrusted us with these precious little ones for a *moment in time*. Even though my son is older now and may feel that he doesn't need me as much, I feel that he needs me even more so now. I find myself sharing more with him. I want to impart more knowledge into him. More times than not, I share the *realities* of life with him. I'm not afraid to share with him when I've *goofed up* and made bad choices.

I often find myself telling him to always ask God for wisdom in everything he does. In our morning prayer before leaving the house, I feel that he sometimes thinks I pray too long. Maybe I do, but I try to cover all bases. You see, I realize God has a purpose for him. I do not mind getting up early mornings, speaking the Word of God over his day and his life. He's worth the sacrifice of me getting up a little earlier and setting the tone for his day. I boldly declare who he is in the earth. I proclaim that he's a person of destiny, character, honor, and so much more. He will be a mighty man in the land! You may think that it doesn't take all of that. Oh, how wrong you are. Do not get me wrong, there are some mornings when things don't go as planned and that's okay. Even during those times, he is still covered by the grace and protection of God throughout the day.

"The Lord shall preserve thee from all evil: He shall preserve thy soul. The Lord shall preserve thy going out And thy coming in from this time forth, And even for evermore."

Psalm 121:7-8, KJV

My son knows that God is for him – not against him. No matter what he goes through or what he does, God's love never fails. The world has already depicted what some kids will do in life or which path they will follow. Let's wake up! Let's prepare our children by showing them that they can have a relationship with God and be effective in this world. They do not have to be what society has called them.

No matter their race, size, or current circumstances - even if this includes being raised in a single parent home - their lives are of value. More than a sacrifice, I consider it a blessing to impart the Word of God to my son. When he was smaller, I spent a lot of time reading the Bible with him. He'd sometimes read back to me. Trust me, it was time well spent. At one time when my son was very little, I was a stay-at-home mom. I'd pray while he'd be in the room with me. He enjoyed me praying in his room or the bathroom. Both places were dark because his room received very little sunlight and there wasn't any sunlight in the bathroom because there were no windows. Sometimes, he would be moving around, and I didn't think that he'd be listening. I would speak over his life and all that concerned me at the time.

One particular day as we were going about our daily routine, he came to me and asked, "Can we go pray in the bathroom and talk to *"The God*"? That was so precious to me! He had been listening after all. He wanted to talk to, *"The God.*" Needless to say, I stopped what I was doing and did just that. Sacrificing a little time to teach our children the value of prayer and establishing a relationship with God is so important. We make time for everything else in life. We'll spend countless hours at football games, the movies, or shopping at the mall. Sure, its family time and we're creating memories, but what are we saying to our kids if they never see us praying or seeking God? These are silent messages that speak volume - at the highest level!

Benefiting from What He Enjoys

My son is a lot closer to manhood and much farther away from the baby that I once held in my arms. From total reliance upon me to the responsible, adolescent he's become; one thing that makes my heart overjoyed is when I see him walk in confidence after an achievement or reaching a goal. He's my investment, and I profit with great satisfaction and fulfillment as I see God moving in his life. God takes pleasure when we prosper. Likewise, we should celebrate, rejoice, and take pleasure when our children realize their potential or perhaps master a very difficult task or assignment.

My son really enjoys the game of basketball. Over the years, I've seen him become a student of the game, and I've seen him develop into a better player. I know the best is yet to come! I am excited as he is focused and masters new skills. He doesn't realize that I'm learning from him. I admire how disciplined he is in practicing his drills on a daily basis. I certainly do not mind the many trips to practice, training, or to his games. This is important to him; therefore, it's important to me.

There was a time when I enjoyed cooking. I was never thrilled, but at one time it was more pleasurable than now. My son knew nothing of eating cold cereal for breakfast on a regular basis until he was about ten years old. I would prepare hot meals every morning, including weekends, and he came to expect them. My mother always cooked hot meals for her family, so I felt that was the thing to do when I had my son. I have prepared my share of bacon (all kinds), biscuits, toast, grits (yes, I said it - *grits*), cream of wheat, waffles, eggs, smoothies, breakfast burritos, and many other breakfast items. Preparing a number of hot breakfast meals seemed to have gone on forever until now! At the present time, my son eats cold cereal at least once, maybe twice each week. I alternate days for hot meals and cold cereal along with some fruit. During my son's elementary years, there were many evenings I'd get in from work, *tired,* but I would help with homework and prepare a full course dinner, sometimes simultaneously. I really didn't mind the sacrifice. I've gotten smarter over the recent years. On most weekends, I'll prepare several meals or main courses to sustain us for the following week. This way, I do not have to be in the kitchen for half the evening preparing dinner.

Listen *young mothers,* not only does God give us spiritual wisdom to raise our children, but He also gives simple natural wisdom (good old common sense). While my son enjoys these home-cooked meals, I reap the benefit of knowing that he is eating healthy and receiving nourishment.

It Comes through Worship

When I remain in a state of worship, I am strengthened. I am no longer focused on my weakness or inabilities; instead, I am focused on God's love and His strength for me. Worshipping God brings so much peace and understanding. As Christians, we do not have to walk around in a state of confusion on a nebulous path going here and there seeking answers for our lives. We have the God of the universe in us. He has the answers we need. In fact, He is the answer. Over the years, I have learned that God is just as eager to answer the simplest form of prayer as the most complex prayers.

He will answer your prayer on how to raise a boy into a man of God, and He will also give you wisdom on how to effectively manage your time. He's a real God with real answers. He instructs. He guides. You may wonder how all of this can come out of worship. Worship is the simple act of love, adoration, and reverence. We respect the opinions of those we admire and love. We trust them, believing the advice they give will help us. Right? It's the same with God and even greater.

Worshipping God *brings clarity,* and it also demonstrates your trust in Him for the things you need. As I worship, I take my natural eyes off of my circumstances and I focus my spiritual eyes on God. I acknowledge that I am not capable but He is able. I listen to Him and *believe* what He tells me. We can go to God with questions, pain, and our issues. Everything that I need hinges on my worship of God. Over time, I've learned that becoming a Godly mother is accomplished by getting in the presence of God time after time. It doesn't come overnight.

Don't think for one moment that God is not concerned with what's going on in your life or your children's lives. Complaining does not help your situation. It certainly does not magnify God.

Go to Him. Start by worshipping Him. Tell Him how awesome He is – how you love and trust Him. Watch Him come through for you. He is a prayer-answering God.

Notes

Notes

Chapter Six

Still Growing

Looking back over the years, recalling all the challenges and victories, I had no choice but to mature and develop in the things of God. I could have withered under the pressures of life and succumbed to the temptations of giving up. I've had many opportunities to do so. Life has a way of presenting obstacles that can either beat us down or cause us to stand tall in full armor and fight. I'm not talking about a physical fight. Through the years, I've experienced some tumultuous times that have brought me to my knees. Down on my knees wasn't a bad place to be because that is where I cried out to God for help. I'd sometimes feel so alone and incapable of moving forward, but when I sought God, I'd gain the strength and found what I needed. In the midst of those chaotic moments, I'd find peace and comfort to continue life's journey.

I've learned that when I exercise my mental and spiritual muscles, then and only then do I pull myself up and grow, reaching a higher level. I am amazed to see how much I've grown as an individual and as a parent. I'm less critical. I am more giving, loving, and understanding. As I mentioned earlier, I am still a work in progress, but at least I'm moving forward. We should never stop growing. Whether you are working on an assembly line in a factory or the CEO of your own company, you should always endeavor to become better each day.

I've always been an avid book reader, but over the years I had slacked up and sometimes went months before picking up a book. I made a commitment to myself to read at least one book each month. I will sometimes read more than one book - at the same time. I love the knowledge and insight that I gain from other people. No *one* person has all the answers.

When we stop reading, we stop learning. This impedes our growth, and a stagnant life is inevitable. I enjoy reading the Bible. It's fascinating and very relevant. Read it – you'll love it! I guarantee that you will somehow be enlightened and even inspired to perhaps do something you've never done before. There, you will find all the answers you need. While finding great pleasure in reading the Bible, I also enjoy reading books that inspire and encourage me to think beyond where I am. A book that I believe offers great encouragement is called, *"The Attributes of God",* written by A.W. Pink. In it, the author points out the characteristics of God and His faithfulness. Another great book that has motivated me is, *"YOU, INC."*, written by Burke Hedges. He explains how we can take charge of our lives by taking control of our thoughts. I am an advocate of positive thinking. It's true that whatever you think - *you become.*

You may be the only parent in the home, but you *can* be effective in raising your children as you yield to that inner voice that guides. Our children will discover, *with or without* our input that life is forever changing and just as life changes, so should they. They will reap the rewards of developing who they are and what they're created for. There's hidden treasure inside of them, and I believe that it is our parental rights to aid in bringing those riches out of them. In helping my son, I am helped. But I can only help him *as I grow*. God will increase *you and your children.* It's a win-win situation!

Another way I help my son to develop is by humbling me and simply being honest with him. There have been times when I've had to apologize to him because I was wrong. Maybe I prejudged a situation or even offended him. I have often told my son that I do not have it all together nor do I have all the answers. I'm human. I make mistakes. We all make mistakes – even mothers. From time to time, kids need to hear us say; "I'm sorry – forgive me" when it is appropriate to do so. It doesn't take away from our ability to guide or parent them. If anything, I believe they appreciate our candid, non-critical approach in communicating with them. As I mentioned in an earlier chapter, they will, at some point, have to forgive us. We really do learn parenting simply by doing it. We learn as we parent. We learn as we *grow*.

Am I still growing? You bet! Will I ever stop growing? Never! There is no end in growing. I want all that God has for me. How about you? Allow God to continue developing you and take you places you've never been before. This can only happen as you yield your whole self to Him – mind, body, and spirit. Do not resist change. Let God prune all the dead things off of you. It's time to cut loose from past failures, bitterness, and bad attitudes because of what have happened. Anything that is not productive and fruitful in your life is dead and has the potential of stopping your destiny and perhaps, your son's.

Remember, God has a plan for you, your son, or any children you may have, and while you're raising them God's way, *He'll elevate you in the process.*

Inspiring Life,

Beverly D. Jones

Notes

Notes

www.ingramcontent.com/pod-product-compliance
Ingram Content Group UK Ltd.
Pitfield, Milton Keynes, MK11 3LW, UK
UKHW040558210726
13854UKWH00008B/1386

9 781105 340697